LAWS OF REST

LAWS OF REST

David B. Goldstein

BookThug
2013

FIRST EDITION

Cover by Catherine Mellinger: "Laws of Rest." Collage on paper, 2013. From the collection of the author. Used with permission.

The production of this book was made possible through the generous assistance of the Canada Council for The Arts and the Ontario Arts Council.

Canada Council for the Arts Conseil des Arts du Canada

ONTARIO ARTS COUNCIL
CONSEIL DES ARTS DE L'ONTARIO
50 YEARS OF ONTARIO GOVERNMENT SUPPORT OF THE ARTS
50 ANS DE SOUTIEN DU GOUVERNEMENT DE L'ONTARIO AUX ARTS

LIBRARY AND ARCHIVES CANADA CATALOGUING IN PUBLICATION

Goldstein, David B., 1972-, author
Laws of rest / David B. Goldstein.

Poems.
Issued in print and electronic formats.
ISBN 978-1-927040-86-7 (PBK.). – ISBN 978-1-927040-97-3 (HTML).
– ISBN 978-1-77166-017-4 (MOBI). – ISBN 978-1-77166-018-1 (PDF).

I. Title.

PS8613.O446L38 2013 C811'.6 C2013-903840-X
C2013-903841-8

TABLE OF CONTENTS

III.

IV.

V.

VI.

In memory of
Jordan Berlant, 1970 – 2002
John Hollander 1929 – 2013

THE MUSES' BIRDCAGE

Many there be that batten in populous Egypt, well-propped pedants who quarrel without end in the Muses' bird-cage.
– Athenaeus, trans. Charles Burton Gulick

O tongue of silence. O first rhymer of knees. This deed they gave me to do, I cannot. Sami Rosenstock, you must help me through it. Edmund Spenser, not you, the other one, the elf, help me through it. Mrs. Wester, thou receding fifth grade teacher of grammar, help me. Black Will Shakespeare, keep your damn distance.

Turn on the light in your bedroom as you would lift an apricot. Your gaze casts its shadow down the street. On it we take our nightly promenade, the crush of us, turning down the piazza, turning from it, sticking like elbows while dreams of olive oil-rubbed skin, the fluttering of moonless scholars, the open-air librarian.

A pavement stone frisks my purse. Down the long lonely metal detector, a vest of rain. The road to Jerusalem is separated night, the peace of others, a common heretics of translation. Seeds litter the floor of how I move. Rub me for luck, for I am dark and speechless. You are known to me by the cracks in my heart.

Choose now, spit out your pit, for time is a voice crying "sign here," and kitchens learn by listening. I was once a seagull, I lived on the sea's border in a bus with one light for every generation. There's no fooling the day's polyps. No compromise version of the document. The year greys and lengthens: it is in love.

I

WHAT LUCY USED TO BE

What Lucy used to be, I now am. Or rather, I accommodate her foibles; they live on in me now that she is gone. For instance: the thin switch of the horse's tail. The barn before sunrise, cold as oats. Trepidation in a nearby thrush. We believe that the dust layering the indoor ring comes from somewhere close by.

After the damage show, during which Lucy won a pink ribbon, we headed to the Amsterdam Pub. Lucy still had on her dressage silencer. I was then just one of her admirers. My only claim to fame was having come up with a slogan for the owls in our local forest: Stronger than Ever! But from that, I was indeed very famous.

I suppose she liked my girlish charm, my key chain of boys. She held the reins absently while the horses grazed in a nearby paddock. Later, on the ranch house roof, we exchanged lockets. When we had sex, it was not exactly life, but more like the Cambridge Companion to Life, with essays of incisive brevity.

I have learned several important lessons from my love affair with Lucy: One: I know no Lucy who does not know me. Two: I am a gentle consumer. Three: I would like this bed to be free of stones if possible. Four: It is better to be a cabinetmaker. Five: When the town doesn't want me anymore, it will say so.

LUCY IN ANOTHER RED SHIRT

Lucy loved my hipring, how it bulgured in the light. With her I could explore my bella hair and other bifurcations of my personality. With her I learned to swim underwater, diving for *objets d'art*, which I'd rough up at the surface. I was a cubicle, always thinking outside myself, remaking my contours with an hourglass.

I don't know how she made me do all the things I hadn't dared try, like run with scissors, or act the part of the changepurse in Medieval morality plays. With her I was always on top of the Classics.... But that was all behind the safety curtain. Later we exchanged bitter words, though even that was sexy. I twirled my bangs.

I think that's what started the idea of her exes writing a guidebook to her psyche: this fountain a must-see, that one not so much. Once I was late and blamed the bus. "Just go through the ritual," she said, "and say you'll never fucking do it again." Over and over, no one included my napkin in the important safety

information or sang the bluegrass song about how he had to poison her catgut wine. We sat at the movies and watched the constellations emerge: Heliocanthus, the Eye. Pargenroy, the Mosque. Imbli, the Marble-slayer, who would have made a great character in a light comic opera, the jump of almond lakes.

LUCY AT THE POOLESVILLE FACILITY

The Poolesville Facility was a laboratory made not of pools but of monkeys, a villain of monkeys and their debris. Lucy was very young, 19, young as a pigtail. She loved monkeys, toyed with them, made them exchange organs and dolls. We conducted experiments of varying degrees of humaneness. We fed the monkeys

alcohol until they became addicted, then gave some of them drugs. I wanted to sleep with the slender grad student with the snake tattoo on her ankle, but she hated me and used to speak nastily behind my back. Instead I engaged in tool-use experiments, watching a monkey named Cruella slide a stick in and out of a

piece of PVC pipe filled with syrup, licking and licking it. Aunt Jemima, no sense wasting the good stuff. Sometimes Lee, a blond WASP-y child of the alpha-monkey, stole the stick and banged it on the pipe. Meanwhile Lucy flirted with some of the higher primates. In dreams that summer my car caught fire, until it

really did, flames licking the hood at Rte #128 and Poolesville Rd. A truck driver beat it out with his leather jacket, told me to drive to a gas station. Later I told Lucy how I ran from the car; she administered a burst of laughter as if humour were a dodge ball. On long drives home I played *Sense and Sensibility* on tape.

BODEGA OF OUR LOVE

On the bed in the hotel, Lucy shows me six ways of being alone. One is to vote by proxy; she is going to vote for the venture capitalist who founded Provender Lithe. The next is the Pull & Seal Security Tinted Envelopes from Staples. The others involve unmentionables that critics have just begun to address.

We had gone on vacation in order to right some of the wrongs at our corner store. Club soda not seltzer, drive-by shootings, hipsters on a Tuesday afternoon who should have a job or some school and less money for fabrics. We began with a hike to the falls, where we swam naked, though not, I don't think, to each other.

Or cigarettes, condoms, Japanese lip gloss, Mexican remedies for diarrhea containing cinnamon. The bewildered violence of packaging. In Provender, we find a painting of a giant Christ being tempted by Satan, spindly Italian cities scattered around. Jesus is saying something; Satan is sooty and wears a skirt.

Carolina rice, pigeon peas, facial tissues made of white burlap. A kind of straw some Africans use to floss; the cousin of the woman at the counter shows me how. Then she strokes my breasts, tries to divine my sex. She smells like eggs. I am an overachiever: I have no shirt and no shoes, yet I am still getting service.

LUCY FIGHTING

I thought I loved her and started bringing up words for her from my treasury. Orangutan and circadian and gilhooly and circule. I only picked the best words, often sewing them into chains and shellacking to keep them fresh. I have given you gilhooly. I have given you stationesque, my training, *ma petite traineur.*

But I had forgotten to ask if you would give me a ride home. I'm not saying I was the innocent victim, though I will admit that to the outside observer.... In my defense, people whose brains have been left to dry tend to develop hair issues. I pulled yours, though less in anger than in the manner of an employment agency,

but it was enough to trip your tiny fuse. You spat back *circadian*, as if it were a burden rather than a gift. Spat *passionated*, spat *lizardic*, spat *murket.* Spat Canarsie, which was unfair, since it's a real place. I did what I'd been taught: stop, drop, and make sonnets. But the fire had reached me, like I was standing still and

you were Seabiscuit, only on fire. During the fight I clutched my groin and defended the skin of my teeth. When it was over and dusk had parsed, I was a tree. Your mouth was on my branches; you loved me with a dirigible's love. "I wanted you small," you said, "so I could wreak you with my jeans."

LUCY'S MACHINE

When I read backwards I fall, get locked in. And backwards is the only way I know how to read. Before I knew her, Lucy was a small girl, a phenotype. She wore red glasses and carried a turnip in her soul the way Frenchmen tuck baguettes under their arms. She was frequently cheerful and had six party dresses.

Last night I dreamed about being on top. She was covered in tattoos, and wiry as an electric outlet. Her hair was a rainbow of sparklies that smelled like Smuckers. My spouse came in and looked pained, but I hardly noticed. When I woke up, I recognized that I had become a pulpy novel, its covers curling in the damp.

Come in, throw the keys on her repainted yard-green table, we're laughing and groping, she listens to the machine while I unwind her scarf, message from the Super about the bathroom tile, and then a woman I've never heard with a singsong accent saying "Rucy I don't RRUV you any more," which is good I guess.

Bother asking? Another of her leather sculptors no doubt. I lie back on her early Dutch chiropodist couch and start coughing up memoir. I was made for this: What would love do without me? Some time ago, I discovered that turnip on the last line of her body and now I fold her back, page by page, weeding.

A RECENT BREAKFAST WITH LUCY

For two hours, rain has chappaquaed the air conditioner which sticks like a hip out the window, flooding the compressor. I replay helplessly the sostenuto of my conversation with you earlier today: Where O where do you get your tomatoes? And I responded, I can't believe you asked me that, you capybara bitch.

Second attempt: O Where O where do you get your tomates? That's what was always wrong with you, your misplaced O. I unpacked my early cherries, for it was not yet tomato season, and gave them to you, just in time for happy rectitudes. A fly the size of my soul flew in and masticated. You'd left months ago, and I didn't miss

you, just the way you fit in the crook of my arm. Why did I never think to write when we were together? Now my language has unionized and I've had to hire scabs and pick them off my skin. As I write this, an ant crawls across the transom; it too is the size of my soul. You were tanned from your trip to the Republic of

Interdictions; you went diving in the Reef of Fists and harvested ablatives, though it is illegal to remove them from the park. Those were my ablatives, I shouted, but that did not go over well, for you recommended Effexor. The art of losing isn't hard to plaster over, you said. I, swollen and calyxed, responded in kindling.

LUCY AT PARTIES

Lucy is dating a boy again, a married boy, my barely married boy she calls him. She calls it "forging connections," thinks of sex as stealing a soul, the way anthropologists steal portraits from natives. "I have yours," she says, "and now I want a matching set." She brings him to one of my parties, the kind where

everyone brings an overdue library book. She introduces him as Jamie; his book is Henri Michaux, so pretentious. "Coarse civilizations spread out their feelings like dishes," he intones. It's not even overdue, he just brought it to show off. Lucy turns so I can see a little of her breast, looks into me and pulls a silk scarf out of

my throat. These are the kinds of openings that crack the spines of books: Lucy turning away, her eyes patting Jamie on the ass, saying well he needed a break from his wife, don't we all, and reminding me of the noise a wet tea bag makes on a glazed cup. "You didn't ask him any questions, not even about Cuba or the

biosphere." I sit down to catch my breath, only I catch another's breath and cram it into my mouth. This climate is the problem, falling every day in sluices through the thick air, so grey it never gets entirely dark, my pansies beaten on the front lawn. In a room off the kitchen, threads of rain weave their cold garment.

II

AIRPORT LIMO LOVE SONG

Jewel Avenue, Astoria and no other. No no traffic makes me this way Van Wyck Van Wyck. Why don't you switch? Which kind of battery? Motorola? The brown one? The flat one? If you remember, you spent fifty dollars for nothing. Hello? Every day in a golden mitt, but it turned out to be just another head cover.

Jewel Avenue, Astoria and no other. My dear, you make one big mistake. You love someone wrong. Life, you know. You show me the phone. Maybe I have it. The spacious one? The one with the canals? The mesmerized one? Wait. Hello? You fucking guy you never call me. I call you you say you call me a hundred times.

My dear I am back. The airport is so far away it could be a potato in the earth. You are so a romantic. If you tell me again I might privilege the rocks of my native land. If you tell me that other thing I will bless you by spitting on your back. I rocked back and forth all day calling you, and my headset spat on the front seat.

You have no idea! You are made of no clue! I am a lover for you, a special lover! Switch to the phone in the street. Your calls are like some clouds off the Van Wyck. I'm still in Queens, not lost fucked city of Brooklyn. This traffic you cannot imagine. What shoe are you wearing? You are not an angel but you are very nice.

RAILROAD CAR WITH MOBILE PHONE AND MAN

Why not answer the question instead of taking me into a maze? I ask you because I will be with my girl, and Connecticut will be with my girl, and I will want to see the house before it is sold. In the morning it will be too late. My mind will be too full to make the journey, and you should know it's because you go to bed early.

I cannot believe you have spoken with her, for she would have given you the keys, and commands don't work unless they are radical. It is damn lonely in this part of the world, and am I not worth two weights, one on either side? My girl is coming with me, do you hear? Larks in a morning I don't even know what to do with.

Yes, and Billy is still a whore, no matter what you say. Flesh of my girl, yes yes, much better than the aqua you can muster. When the house is sold it will be in the form of a phone call, for it will sell me under the bed. I cannot believe you are arguing with me in fucking Bridgeport. There is a ferry here, for God's sake.

Fine, I will not start with you, for the starting is all around if you look. I will speak with her, I will be in her and without her, yes. We will discuss my coming home only after I take that call. Do you hear? The question is am I coming home. In the morning it will be too late; if you knew how to listen you would know.

PENN STATION TO 122ND STREET, 3 A.M.

I look at myself first and ask always, am I presentayble? I am always ready to criticize myself first. Say four chicken wings. Say it's pizza. First you have to say, are they pigs or are they human beings? They drive by and they hold their nose. Say for chicken wings they never take a piece of wood. They are dirtier than us!

I don't care if you are two trillion times richer than me, with you hundred dollar this and you one hundred seventy five this, you watch and you ring and you tie and you this, you simulcast and you brachiopod, you foreign chicken wings and you pizza. They never take a piss on wood. They dirtier, their dirty sneakers.

They think they can wear anything. I never seen such hate. It is like we drop a nuclear bomb somewhere. I am always ready to criticize myself first, I ask myself, are they presentayble? They stand on the street like we are blind, like they are inside the eye, like they form chicken wings from pure Haiti, their dirties full

of hate, and they say, you can hear them walking along the synonym and pretending. I tell I never read it in the Laotian Dictionaire. I never read it in the Cozumel, I never read it in the Sparagmos Booklet, I never read it in Piazza. They look at us like we are forked chicken wings, and I ask myself, I ask.

ERRORS OF THE APOLLINARIANS

Walked out of the apartment one morning into the mind of my landlord. Moody piano music, the lease made flesh. Outside Pauline's Pizza, had a cataract of beers and joked about bedding. Paid the piper and skeedaddled, taking the five hacksaws to a safe, undisclosed location. Awoke next evening knee-deep in cavities. Got it pulled.

Especially when there's a vacancy the moon came in close. Even the well-known violences were wearying of the anthology. Tried for days to sell the lights. Left in disgust. Broke open the health boxes, made confession. One day we'll get it back, Alypius, but until then, hunt down the snowpack and pray for the bouquet of souls.

In the meticulous valleys a kind of cardamom grew. We had removed their little green stems; the gamble paid off, and everyone confused them for our own. Wept into the haberdashery of earthly life. Handbled into the forest partisans, wanted their incontinent anthem and ate it. Saw nothing moving on the horizon of the law.

The baby fired out like a soybean. Strolled empty of insomnia for once on a Sunday night, peering into cormorant shacks and making love with each owner. That was before property began to be blent, before we had to sign in order to be heard. Whenever I pulled focus, you, Alypius, broke it upon the emerald pavement stones.

EDWARD'S LAMENT

I saw Spencer and Baldock climb out of the bracken, on the way to no good. Retching sounds off in the forest, peasants gathering vetch and hellebore for tomorrow's feast. Of all the times you lost sight of me, this one was the scariest: dark creatures at midday, demanding I give back the playscript. Imaginary theatres

with real guns in them. Yes, now they are coming for me. We should never have made a deal, even with the casino sexing us up. Oh prince among prices, pine among prigs, how did you misplace the volume when you knew how much it meant to me? It's true, sweet Galveston, whence the last wave of immigration.

Oh were it false! You're nothing but another Stetson-wearing Jewish animal cracker if you think I can be pressed between pages and live. My power resides in singularity. You offer me no nook or corner. Searching for a life, I found a period. I speak to you in the dulcet tones of Oklahoma: I from my picture am banished.

We could play some scenes from Ovid before I go. You on your hermaphrodite, running and banking. Me the snake. Your heel on the root's end, I move in an ecstasy. Remember the Alamo, where we puffed open our chests? Remember me won't you, fuzzy minion? In this century, every loaf of bread is black.

ISOLATED NOTES OF THE EPITOMATOR

Chickpeas, my love, are a dessert you would give to a godforsaken monkey. He used drapery with nothing of his father's determination. Long fall off the flower, but she was not insulted. It's a darkness, and darkness, a mango-tango, all natural, and full of it. Bromide, you fool! Well, that all depends on if we remember 'em.

A doublet, such as the Song of the Sea. I don't know if you meant to do that, but the wind strops in the first canto. It does not cascade, or hitch. The second movement was Oprah's fist hitting his gullet. Child, *I* recommend your daily allowance, not you. Every time we visit is like a spider holding everything she loves with her legs.

You have forgotten my birthday more times than I've had one. My intimacy with you is exhaustible. She ran into his arms. The license plate? SRNITY. That was the best part. The carnality is quite good, but I'm easily oppressed. They were hammering out the pond. An invitation. Sure, if you don't mind vegans fixing your carburetor.

Never again would I be so explicit, so impassioned, at a literary conference. I do not believe you, or do not believe you did. It was dark, and the blacker's ink was over my clothes: well-envisioned children binding each other with withes. You know we still have that book. Fly out there and embrace him like a brother.

SRNITY: A DOUBLET

A Song of the Sea. In the first canto, isolated darkness strops an intimacy. More darkness, godforsaken, explicit wind, but with an allowance for day, like a spider giving birth. Long notes give out onto cascades. It is full of a natural and binding determination, an oppressed tango, if you will. I do not believe it has been done.

The second movement is not as well-envisioned, but it is impassioned and I recommend you visit it. First, a flower steps down a child's gullet. It loves her like a fool, holding everything so inexhaustibly that she runs into the arms of the epitomator every time. The flower is insulted, but gets an invitation to embrace on *Oprah*.

Forgotten, she becomes a vegan and fixes carburetors. Sure, it's a literary bromide, but she has a license to use a hammer on drapery, clothes, plates, and so on. The best part is the conference where she falls in love with chickpeas and a mango. The carnality depends on if she remembers her brother. Well, it's out there – the book's

quite good, but there are hitches. Or, her father's a monkey, all fists and legs. She's hitting withes when he flies in for dessert. He believes his children now, but all for nothing. Never again will they mind each other as easily.... You know I meant to have time in here for more ink. Then, dark again, and blacker over the pond.

AENEID, BOOK 21, LL. 270-291

Then the old paragon rose and spoke: "Until this week we had the luxury of playing with language. Now, everything is suddenly the same. We must use words, my *compañeros*, to construct juggernauts of play. We must dismantle the family – you know which one – using these edifices. Only then will our children's

earnings and our well-muscled young men be safe. Until this week we could play in the fields of bombs. Now we crenellate or die." Thus he spoke, and thus the initialed generals responded: "Under my tree is a swing set. Read me back the rain and I will join the quest. In the underworld it is not like this. In the underworld we

make faces on cold windowpanes and crave hot chocolate and grass. Take us back where we are allowed to use the word 'loam'." The old paragon walked back inside the Temple Theatre, where "The Girl of the Sunny South" was in rehearsal, Dido playing the lead. "The gods decree an attack of the bends at daybreak."

Then spoke Dido, unlucky in love: "Show me a terrorist and I will show you a bibliography of calluses. Render your bosses if you like, but my religion no longer answers to fire's quick service. Show me another way to read the dance, and I will spend my old age tearing into ribbons of energy the desert altars."

III

CAFECITA

The poem walks into the Cuban restaurant on the Avenue of Old Students and reintroduces itself to former-English-major Leila and her caramelized mouth. The poem polishes off a plate of Manny Three-Eyes: three fried eggs atop black beans and rice, beef picadillo, and two thin plantain slices sweet enough to break a train.

It is crunch time at the nap store, where the poem works, and it's come in here to relax for a moment, maybe have a cigar or guitar. It usually orders a tostada de lengua, remembers the time it ordered a glass of chocolate milk at a macrobiotic retreat, keeps eating and descends into the valley of love quietly in a corner.

The band plays Buena Vista Social Club covers like the one with two fiddles, a bass, and a burning house. "Hey, what are you about," asks one of the six Gretchens, who's reading the *Times* and trying out love with a Raoul. The poem draws a white breath and tries to explain something about a smear marketing

sheep named Elijah. I'm about a girl who builds anomalies with her band of plucky friends. I came into existence to work out why black pepper is America's ubiquitous spice. I am equally about eating and watching. Replies the Gretchen: "If you were a body I would put you in my purse and climb your bright hair."

HARDSHIP PAY

The bombing of Guadaloupe resulted in casualties of a natural scale. Authorities were hurt and asked why we did not love them the way we used to, all night behind the pineapple trees. That's how I arrived here, at this historic expedition. I am the spy in charge of fog collection, and not one droplet escapes.

Today it is warm as a paragraph, the meteorologist naked, seduced. We will never know how it feels to be him. When asked to comment, he befouls the place and the dogs start. I don't wish, however, to imply that he had anything to do with my version of the story, which is that the flagstones gave themselves up and hugged.

A faint pounding. A brace of leather ladies held us up in their armrests and rubbed as they'd rubbed for centuries; the poets of my generation stopped reading, knelt before them, and passionated. What else, given these facts, would you have me do? All the while, New Paltz blazed meteoric across the foregone sky.

It was perhaps the end of the world, and I said, "If I could tapdance, do you think I would do it with you around?" You were on the floor looking for your kaleidoscope screw. "Dictate the story," I pleaded. I was standing up, looking out at history. You called on the red phone: "I see you, but I love you anyway."

SHOW

One year after the Indian Ocean, the Paratactic Sea swept the nation and its dance became a Broadway standard, rife with the illusions that have thrilled audiences from time immoral. That was before the Ice Age, as it still is. We were almost too desperate, and watching each spectacular kick uploaded tenderly to the net,

we knew we'd never be this happy again. Of course we had known about the genesis of the show, the six chairs situated upon the farm after years of fruitless negotiations, but we never expected such beauty. We read the reviews of the Kabbalists and set fire to the papers that contained them. Through such trying

times, Javier and Chandry were indispensable, keeping us entertained with their housefly minstrelsy. We worked on our foam bicycles and tried not to go outside, all the while trying to restore physicality to our education. Empty streets were fine, but the show's popularity had made it hard to keep track of the crowd's midriff

explosives. French gardens take a long time to heal, and we'd rather not break an ashen regulation, even if it supports our city. When will it end? How many times do we have to buy the book before it buys us? Meantime the cruises keep leaving and the night markets flower with cuttlefish. All three of our students want to talk.

PAYSAGE

It was the season in which the paparazzi lie fallow in the field and insects beat against the low rice walls. The lovemaking of which I have spoken with some bitterness was finally concluded. At the close of their exertions, the Mercedes family owned every imaginary house you could see. If you do not believe me,

ask the shapely dark leg of the waterstrider. Your insistence angers them, truth be told. They had wanted a share of the flax particulates, and now were forced to acknowledge that your understanding did not include them and that they would suffer for this omission. A bird flew overhead in the shape of a bucket of water.

You made up your mind with mascara and circled the campus looking for the rest of us, but found no parking on account of the funeral. We'll have to return to you later, as you returned to us that summer, a river of your former self. Euclid never had it so good, was our undeniable but unprofitable conclusion at that time, though

we were forced to revise it over coffee during the week we were still alive. I've never seen a falcon tear the roof off a service in quite that way. They say that only when the sun is mishandled does it speak of God, yet the midtown Holiday Inn was the scene of much revelry. I can only guess at what made the rest of it vanish.

GOLDEN YEARS

And yes it was a cold night on the bay. Something endless out there, gnawing steadily at the moorings. I wanted to know why you had called the Gulf Coast the Golf Course when we were flying over it, over the ratchet and its flight. You always did have a way of maintaining. I was a victim of gross negligence

as usual, an accomplice of the stars that weave bamboo. A dark film over everything, as if we were running along the rim of a green teacup. Summer was a cold winter everywhere that year, not just the breaking fog. When my grandmother passed on, she left me that cup, stained with the enamel of Florida.

Loeb, Mendes, and Kohut took our case straight to Redbook. While they meant well about it, it was hard to find a clean chair to sit on. The word "harmonic" was on the lips of all the experimental musicians. There was a lot of greenery in the retirement village to cover for a lack of children, but crabgrass is almost food.

When my grandmother came back north she found the medicine for longing, but not for her arthritis. The world shrinks not just in winter. The small apartment glittered with a life of mid-weight collectibles. It is a life you do not find in China. I was tiny, and the new vehicular growth considered me without equivalence.

PLANET

"It was the way the ruined moonlight fell." It was the way the monastery ached into existence. It was the way opprobrium is usually the fault of the consumer. It was the way you made it yourself. It was the way of containment. It was the way of volume, the way of body, the way it was dead, the way it merely flipped.

It was the way of the geisha Satellite. It was the way of the word and its hurtle. It was the way of the modern canon, the way a ham can turn golden in an afternoon. It was the way of the valley and the way of the mountain passes. It was the way when you made it you owned it, the way of the most economical potter's wheel.

It was the way he made the pass, the way you were passing. It was the way the ruined moonlight fell. It was the way of the attack of the killer. It was the way a parody devours itself and it orts. It was the way an expedition on the high seas used to be able to see everything: the lands of ice, the phantasms of roving souls.

It was the way of the right of return, the way it reduced the night. It was the way citizens leapt from the brink. It was the way of the orts of ice, the attack. It was the way of the everyday. It was the way of the sleepless, the way of bricks long fallen, the way they supported you after the incident, the way speech became intolerable.

FELDSPAR

Christina lived life on her own terms.
– General Hospital

Objectives: 1. Students will face the facts. 2. Guests will be rewarded. 3. Even a dog can understand dogs. 4. By the end of this film strip, you will find burnt sienna lodged in you. 5. Your rewards are waiting. 6. Take a moment to look through the materials. 7. You can imagine what Leonora accused him of doing.

In Geraldo's Afghanistan it was called enamel and retractable. But I call it a train with a big fat key and a mortar. Others will call it by its social security number; don't be fooled. Words flashed by in loops, punctuated by tones that crazed the dogs. Then Dr. Feldspar splitting, like some grotesque mitochondrion, his sides.

The desperation of taking those silent, sensuous teenage aliens onto the sound stage! Yeah, we did that. Yeah, we were all broken up. The FBI composts? Not in my backyard. Those are some of the things we used in order to know when we are fine literature, and when merely fine. Ah yes, Feldspar said, and dribbled sea.

You can imagine what Leonora. When I was young, a few chunks of the stuff lodged in my brain. How delightful! Ebulus: *The Defectives*. Feldspar: it is goddamned everywhere. They even *make* it. So what if it's in my plumbing? That was around the time my application for passport by mail circled and broke free.

PERMITTED TO RETURN

According to the striking formal invention of feldspar. Upper granite, a record of demoiselles. There were six kinds: Berenice, Booth, Fletcher, Townsley, Evelyn, Ireland. Men, wives, illicit lovers, sheep, dynamiting silver and chiselling trails, usually glassy and moderately hard, blocky. I do not know what the lupine wants.

Feldspar is a tiny room of femaleness, and it is blocky but on fire. Within the range of light, the unglazed waterfall is propelled by lateen sails. A bridal veil factory. Dr. Barney the geologist uplifted onto the rock and gargled. He is rewarding, flexible, personal. He is as sexy as a physicist. You can have it all.

I was standing on a fairly large group of clinical wonders. I was sighted like the batholith, suddenly Plutonic. I echoed, but big deal. On a weathered surface, feldspar is chalky and gives life, it is the rock made field. Easily cleaved, but not on your account, into a meadow you may have as a privilege.

I could get more potassium from a banana, but the windswept sparkle of my boot is for you, my only poet. If only there were space for me on the edifice, feldspar, antithesis. You were everywhere. A man carried a mattress up Mount Vogelsang. To be given autumn, or to appropriate it. Marmots, under cover of dawn.

IV

D'OU VIEN DONC LE GRAND ASSEMBLY?

Written on the back of a 17th-century recipe book

First, concerning the primary importance of the definite article, we divined it was this, the individual, that marrowed our thoughts. We opened the white vellum book of remembrances, binding it to our fingers in diary form. In the book of short remembrances we found clear cakes made of plague, sent down by the king.

In 1705 Elizabeth Freke's husband, married a most grievous rainy wet day, first complained of shortness of breath; survived, though Dr. Jeffryes was unable to bleed him. Freke was aided by several courses of turpentine physick; murdered a short while later. The last he saw was shadows of several bodies, evening light fissured the corn.

The sought individual: a voice or form yet ahead, packed in sand like the Seville oranges in the cellar. Viscuous gasps pack full the children who have dressed for God. The man midwife said my son would have to be taken out of me in pieces. If the writing is unclear, it may have been cancer or smallpox, or the difficulty of the hand.

There is no second because there is no duel, only a dark crowd of what has already been written down an English lane. She lay in her coffin a long time before getting up to call her cook. Lady Norton has my son preserved in gooseberries. She gave me a recipe to make Hog's puddings, but I usually soak my guts in rosewater overnight.

HOW TO MAKE CELESTIALL GELLY

Take a pickle of scientifics and two pair of halves. Seethe. At my request, take out your salad between the claws then waste materials in two or three variants. But a lot of green might be worried about you. Thus ossify power in water's gems. Boil and give very tender glue. Let the liquor bite naked till it be very cold. Pare off top and bottom.

You put to it half a pint of rosewater but Jackson is enough. Sugar it with muffins bent double in profusion, you put in 6 dropped from a height. The only requirement is that they are boiling. Guiana and purples of ginger, and a gleam. Also a groat of musk. Pore over all, rubbed in a basin boiled to go-getters. Nipple your museum.

Pay your fast day, lay out all the bottoms and a pound of fun butts, but throw out four sugars giving but a little to the root. Boys made of cabbages in water and salt. You drained, you water, you lakes. Pottery also lays your lakes. The curator out of his marrow seasons with ginseng and as before you horror it until it is tapas.

Put in a surfeit of loneliness. Add vermillion. It is up and life, glories for drug is all out and given pounds. New string clogging it in a flood, my pot buds on top of an andante composed welcomes. Give sharper food, but keep it food till it lay out and cold. Let it stand, tell it that it should be good Aukland and fire four. Serve it.

HOME

What I like more than anything
Is to visit other islands...
– George Oppen, "Ballad"

Louis XIII threaded morels on his deathbed because he had done it all his life. You've read about it in books. You read: "The old house on Charleston Street is gone now, and the peeling yellow wallpaper in the tiny apartment where I was born. Observe the backyard where Betsy Jenkins and I played, the discredited medlars.

"Our neighbourhood was called Long Reach, so I thought for years that a reach was an inland beach with sidewalks for a shore. The burdock menace. Leaving, we sold high to muskrats. In the new house we found a porch and cuneiform in the furnace. Once we had a blackout played on instruments of Washington glass.

"Oh the embarrassment of a happy childhood. The ambushed piano quoted late Shakespeare. Miles of afternoon sun without federal approval. Digging in introductory gardens, I learned to fear the delicacy of gyromitra, for it is a caricatured form, a restitute friend. I got used to the sweetbreads on my tongue.

"It's true: we practiced signatories while others travelled. Or else the matchstick donkeys. I looked for tragedy on every starlet. I crawled on the floor of tired government. I lowered to the east, the way I'd been taught. Then one day my hands changed into snowflakes, and I caught every word in my mouth."

CHARLESTON STREET

A restitute friend on his deathbed, the peeling yellow medlars. I sold the embarrassment of a happy childhood, practiced piano, caught snowflakes while matchstick donkeys travelled the sidewalks. Home. What I like more than anything is the backyard I read about in books, where Betsy Jenkins and I played.

Every word in my mouth was an inland beach in afternoon sun. In the tiny, discredited apartment we found cuneiform; against the burdock menace I quoted late Shakespeare, the way I'd been taught. You learned all life is a caricatured form. Muskrats in the furnace. Gyromitra, like Washington, is no true morel.

Louis XIII threaded signatories on the floor of his tired government. For years a blackout played to the east. Certain of his long reach, without congressional approval, he ambushed gardens, glass instruments, a porch. Leaving our neighborhood, I was born to visit the lowered tragedy of starlets and their islands.

The old house gone now, we observed the new house and its high wallpaper. I looked for sweetbreads. Then one day my hands changed into my tongue, and I thought to fear the delicacy of digging. We said goodbye, we got used, we others, who reach for a home on every shore. Yet I read on, and once I crawled.

WINDOWS WRITTEN IN YOUTH

Howbeit the scrub, someone is walking through it. I always thought this moment would come, but now that it is finally here I find no more verbs. I find that all I have done has been preparation for this day: the insects keening on Milford Street, or smoking with the Italian Pocahontas in theatres owned by her father.

All except the vinyl sweater and the insistence of boll weevils, which were never much help. You who live, what have you made of your luck? I was a twig, a jai-alai filmmaker. I was a handful of what passes for orangery on High Tor Hill, that was my greatest achievement. I was water before the first car drove into it.

It is still coming through the scrub, folding up the land behind into brisk, wounded wood. It comes closer, and I can see now that I am on a train, that I am thoroughly. The great farms of the Mercedes family hang above me in the maroon mist. Someday I will go to them, and be able to walk my arts and crafts in angst.

Phase II: it comes toward me and the gulf widens. It is ninety-eight per cent common sense. In its gait I see myself at age ten, hanging off the stile and plucking milkweed with my teeth. Apparently it has come home at last. Well fine, I am ready to be the indoor waterfall. If waiting is a truck, I will take mine black.

WINDOWS WRITTEN IN YOUTH II

At age ten my gait was all preparation. Walking through the scrub on High Tor Hill, I was a waterfall in waiting. The gulf of the modern widens in me! This, I owned, was thoroughly living. I thought through a mist of what would someday be my greatest achievement: Filmmaker? A Mercedes? I was asking for it.

Now I find myself scrubbing jai-alai hardware for *her* father. Italian, artless, she was ninety-eight percent someone I could come home with. Walks in the wood, where I wounded more verbs than there apparently are. The blackened theatre where we saw *Pocahontas* with her relatives. In my first car, finally, smoking.

Toward day, we drove past Milford Street, and came at last to the great farms, their insects and boll weevils. Behind the stile, plucking a handful of twigs, we hung out at an indoor orangery. Howbeit, I saw the family above me in the milkweed, keening through their teeth. I will go to them, I said, I will take what's mine –

But you were never much help. I see now that I was a phase. It is common to live in the moment, but now, before, and always, in the sense of your sweater folded on the vinyl of my truck I find angst, insistence. I am ready, except that the land is fine, and my crafts are hanging by the water. The train comes. I see myself off.

PINKY THE BEAGLE

Sew the trees and wear lamplight. Plish out the stew in the first-class cabin, use only gold monikers to serve the platinum fliers. Let me tell you what you're gonna have for dinner tonight, *communista*. An omelette hidden from its ham, ricotta made with Chinese clouds. All of it can be found in the velvet monastery you won as a prize

along with Pinky when you were a young shaven-headed girl. Oh Pinky the Beagle, where have you gone? Pinky the Beagle, won't you come back to me? Pinky the Beagle, frolic here in the fading light of afternoon, the desolation of evening, in the ocean Pacific, in the ocean Atlantic, beneath the jigsaw waterfalls of stone.

Kinky the Beadle, you were my only piece of steam and made landscapes real to me for the last time in my career. I stitched my chest and walked with you, I acted in movies where you played the role of hands, I brought you tears and habits, and you reciprocated with camel groats, the treat of soap opera stars. When I got sick

with pencil fever, you took notes. When I inhaled beach towels, you opened furry laughter upon me, upon radiance, upon the love that apprises the winter duvet. You were design and upending, the good kind of vicious, taking the other dogs down to hell in a coal cart, oh my pinky winky slinky dinky, my can-can blanket.

XERCES BLUE

Xerces blue, Acmon blue, *Iridaceae*. Appalling blue, restoration blue. Matrilineal blue, hydraulic blue, grasses in a blue rage. Dune grasses speak blue. Blue body, all over fingers blue. There is no blue that does not see you. Kerchief blue, palatalized. *Lessingia* blue, Blue Lobos Creek, San Francisco. Extinction blue.

Carapace blue, colour of money. In 1994, a thin strip of land. Weed blue. Blue of transference, alone blue. Flows down to the sea under a baseball-blue field. Extirpation blue, Pheres blue, high-traffic interpretive. Pickleweed seed out of the acid ocean, *Salicornica* blue on blue. We'll wait for the evergreens to die.

Gossamer blue beyond city limits. The monk-blight city, the state's rarer plants. Phases of restoration, political blue, Xerces blue, the extinct, the blue the world no longer conjures. Rat blue. The vast return of tomcat clover. A quarter stuck in the sand. Scale blue, mitigation blue. Autumn of dogs, seed collars. Code blue.

Remnant blue, blue endemic. The relatives of undevelopment. Presidio manzanita barely. Shade blue. Hazardous waste, a blues tune: 80,000 pounds, beach-strewn. Lobos blue flowers down to the sea. There is no blue that does not. Dispersion blue, lucky construction crews laid new pipe. Lost blue. Hypothetical blue.

V

AIN HALEV

Whatever became of the garden? The badgers, I remember, had the look of trees doing the washing, and the trees had not yet learned what badgers looked like. You were there, growing bits of ocean. Just off to the right, where I couldn't watch you. You were blessed the way city lights are blessed, one after the other.

You'd had enough of the future, but it insisted. You raised your nucleated arm. You broke off truths as you walked and dangled them in your teeth. You were an unwept tale waiting to happen, a prompt train on an unpublished schedule. You crumbled at the first sign of the police, used worms as tools to get back your baggage.

Night gathers in the fists of books. Everywhere you look the new country is blowing itself up in a springtime of beach glass. I don't know what I was thinking when I said those things; let's find a history we can both eat. Pendulous and barbonic, you tend to your coins of water. One day I'll see you with all my eyes.

After the breakfast dancing you used up your teachers. You stood staring all the rest of the day at fields flickering on the wall. As one of your tended iron shards, I felt I could speak to you, using the model of those guavas out on the cliffs. You looked past me. The weight of the jellied world between us, we set out wandering.

from THE BOOK OF EGYPT

All this time a skin stretches across the sea, the skin of science and the skin of art, stretched over the curdled sea. The sea blows south in long lines of wings that overhang the city, and then the long mountains and plains wrinkling over the earth. You try walking over the skin, but inside you it goes down to pots of bone.

Your pursuers overtook you in the narrow places: as the text tells us: the text is our home. When there was no instruction, you built walls, your skin glowing like an oven. Your skin glowed in the places where it was worn away, and the sea wore your skin in the dark. A place to which you are called, where you gather and

barter treasures, your gold or flecks of delphinium, to stay alive, and the blithe interruptions, but you are called there nonetheless. The sea is no refuge; it can tear on its seam at any moment. It is no less alphabetic than wilderness with its long divorce of steel. And you must pay to drink your own water, it fills you up but

you are a pottery assemblage and so you leak, it is a privilege to spill into the earth, it means that you have met more than you can carry, that you have kept yourself alive. If your bones were spilled by a sudden fall, it may simply mean that you are speaking, and your speech needs to get out onto all that white fire.

WATERS OF JERUSALEM

We were doing the pyjama dance, throwing our arms up in the air and singing Ay-yay-yay-yay! when Waters of Jerusalem called. We were watching West African movies, entering an all-night birthday haze, when Waters of Jerusalem called on the little red phone, calling us back at all the worst times, call us back.

First the small pools called: ritual baths of the Herodian quarter, dry for two thousand years. Then the secret pools: Pool of Siloam, tunnel of Hezekiah, whose water still eludes the Assyrians. The fountain of al-Kas lists its cisterns, its people cut off from its ablutions. Sultan's Pools called, and the Pool of Mamilla.

Spring House wants Jeremiah the prophet chained again in her depths. The Valleys of Jehoshaphat and Kidron are an intermittent river. The Spring of Gihon ponders its twisted pomegranates, departed flocks. Faucets of West Jerusalem, leaking water from Turkey and shrapnel from Jenin; faucets of East Jerusalem, running hopeless.

The women of Jerusalem swear by the wild field doe not to rouse us until we are cleansed. Your sweetness is the sweetness of a bee on a journey, and I follow you along its old walls. Light my way like a bee, bring me to Waters of Jerusalem, which are not to be forgotten. Thrive in me, flock of my heart, my love.

STONES OF JERUSALEM

Everyone lies about Jerusalem. In a poem called "Bonfires of West Jerusalem," set in the lag of the oneiric year, black-clad children count down to a greater burning. This morning in a poem called "Does the sun love Jerusalem?" a woman hung her wash. Even with all the Dead Sea skin care products, it's damned lonely

in our part of the world. Once – tell me the story again? – we wandered into the poem "Pillars of smoke" and were blinded. It doesn't count until someone cracks open their coffee and listens. In a poem entitled "What the East Jerusalemite had for breakfast," there's not much more to go on: a few wrinkled olives, the world's

most delicious cucumber, two helpings of goat's milk yogurt. Current is supplied to the poem by the East Jerusalem Power Company, Ltd., whose plant rusts on the road to Ramallah because it buys electricity from Israel. In the poem "Jerusalem's Refugee Camp," the water comes from the middle of the night. One poem always

knew this, another recently discovered it, the third was a UN escapee who spoke gibberish. An Israeli entered the camp in a poem called "The most heavily armored car in the territories is a 1988 Subaru driven by a Palestinian." When he came out, the women waved gaily, and left packages of fire on the back stoop.

CHEMICAL FIELD

Is: to breathe. Is: the sharpener. Often tried, was permitted rarely, to return. Returned every day for a brief onus. Thoughts I picked up from Confusion: acorn transformed into grain. The farmer brings his heat to the crops. Returned to the ground-eating clouds, the white powder, liver-eater. Returned to the city cellars.

The descriptive functions generally have to be watched. Observation is, at no time, permitted. The bombs did not explode but crimped. What we know as the world is merely to get things started: the road to Jerusalem goes through Kurdistan. I could not remember my sons. Smell of garbage, of sweet apples, of eggs.

Oddly sweet odour of sulphur. The birds come down, too easily. He was lying on his side trying to drink his mask. Must be handled as a series of objects in a field. Attempted to get back to the word, lived in the printed cancers. In each generation, ergot, mustard, aflatoxin. Halabja, the Kurds, merely to get things started.

Sentence was first cannister of language; we are all caught in its dying. Merely hearing will give you secrets. The use of a human. Reverence urged me to the meadow: three years later, a skeleton still holding his tractor keys. It had a dying fall, the sweet sound that breathes upon a bank of violets, stealing and giving odour.

NARROW PLACES

You were there, too. Chickens pecked at damp straw. Also you remember a basket of tomatoes, though they had not yet reached that part of the world, and a pineapple held aloft, armoured against the sun like a bomb in a car. Salmon leapt through the slick air, and somebody carried a hyrax, furred friend of elephants.

When you got down past the beach, you had to walk single-file, could reach out and touch each wall of water. Some did and were flung up into the sunlight and into the maws of monsters, you never saw them again, invariably they were the relatives you liked best. You tripped over some of the cattle, got your feet wet.

At the other side the patient Egyptians helped you out of the water, split open the salmon, pulled up stools and logs for the feast. They offered their limbs to eat, and you offered yours, as decorum requires. Merged, overseer and overseen, jaws blood-drenched, you took up timbrels, happy as clams at high tide.

Next day, it was nothing but the wide desert. In the walking breeze, you amused yourselves trading memories of future homes: the long vineyard, the edible book, the fire escape. From back in the line, someone took up a song about railroads. At the first hint of oasis, a leftover crocus poked its way up through the sand.

FUTURE CROCUS

High tide. Down past the beach, a wall of sea, first hint of salmon flung into the sunlight. You and the Egyptian, trading tomatoes and relatives in the breeze. The patient vineyard with its stools and logs. Hyrax took water into their maws. Chickens too, leftover monsters you could reach out and touch and hold aloft.

The desert was nothing but memories: lines of cattle, basket of bombs. Also you remember the single file of railroads in the overseer's narrow places, the drenched decorum of the overseen. When the armoured stones reached your part of the world, invariably limbs and limbs were split open. Walking at end of air, pecked oasis.

You had amused yourselves with the damp straw of song, were book-happy. Clams were edible; you liked best how the furred elephants poked their feet in your car. There is a way through what is taken. After the sand got inside you, you pulled up what you had to do. Somebody carried a friend of yours through the sand.

The salmon helped you at the wide jaws of the other side. You never saw them again, though they were not yet. Back inside, you tripped and walked wet, each to each. The eaten pineapple, the escape out of fire and into home. Sun leapt through the slick watercourses, like the feast of timbrels in the days always to come.

LAWS OF REST

Examine your clothing before going out, for you may be carrying something without knowing it. Do not place a wick into a bowl of oil, for then the oil will be drawn up and you will promote burning. Do not light with cedar bast or uncombed flax. Are you Nahum the Mede? So do not light with boiled tallow.

Do not stumble around in the dark. But if you turn out the light because you fear idolaters or melancholy, you will not be held liable. Follow significance: examine your clothing. Do not turn out the light to spare the wick, it is you who needs to be spared. Right now someone makes peace on the height where wine is breaking.

Where you see the word *children* instead read *builders*, for we are "our fathers' children, our grandchildren's ancestors," and laws rip from walls. Have you tithed? Have you drawn a line around your house? Have you left the cedar bast under its bark? Have you stumbled in the dark? Yet evidence exists for silk.

These are the thirty-nine generative acts of labour: to make two loops, to erase two letters, to trap a deer, to seek out the wars of God. Think of yourself as an amputated leg and do not go out carrying your stump. Think of yourself as pebble enough to cast at a bird. For this you are liable: bone enough to make a spoon.

VI

STUYVESANT TOWN
for Mindy

It rained for three months under the porticoes of memory: umbilical rain, columns of cells in thick migration, their suspended state held in place by threads of jobs and grappa. The bildungsroman was delicious – I ate it for breakfast as Neapolitan students hargled "You live! You learn! You live! You learn!" on the floor below.

Sometimes one has to live the past to get to the present: it's in the congressional record and in spring's terrified green, leaving us equivocally at sea telling stories about the land. I am happy when I am with you under the mosquito netting reaching for each other's alveoli, lustily playing what might be rummikub,

englishing each stream (somewhat hampered by the way something moves across bodies—the globe of anxiety that makes a copse of poplars where no poplars ever were). But we are past the mudbrick martini and the friends' plebiscite, skipped those steps, now reaching the couple's cooking class and knee-deep in the other's

groundwater. Within reach we discover a tapestry of leaves and grown ink, musical skin of the wrist letting go of the past's fourth hour and its fifth. Waking to nudegreen you, lascivious bucket of breakfast cereals, shall we daze through the survey of wild aquifers, or the book of light wanting? Today or tomorrow?

FISCAL YEAR OF DREAMS

Mutual funds at a low ebb, forced to live in small rooms among languages with strict word order, cellphone down to 200 anytime tidbits including customer versus; X. called, remembered her as having bought me *The Slim Book of Midrashic Women* and as having put the "orc" back in divorce; shunted to voice

pail. Went to the doctor for the medical conditions I'd been promised; she pronounced me "an entire meaning." For days I went bundled in woolcakes and stored my sweaters in the oven, well over my credible limit. Even amid the collapse of the home markets she was adorable with that spider bite on her head.

Based on all the earlier stratagems, I set up a database that chewed up every digit and balled on Thursdays. Sexual practices became a kind of nature. When I got wet, I tended to dry myself off or eat grape nuts: where the milk is. Absorbed in fundraising for shadow puppets of doom, I did not at first notice you moving in.

Interested in appliquéing for a charge card, in cornrigs and barleyrigs, in the way your skin turns unexpectedly into milk. Maybe ready to put money in the riverbank and issue statements. At first it felt like the final product, but later we became a smaller way of minding the body, because foursquare is but a girl's age.

MY LIFE IN LONDON

A bright day in London, meaning light grey. Down at the Bridewell they are putting on *Henry VIII* for the Queen's Golden Jubilee, royalty plus anxiety about genre. A bright day which by evening is tired. Crushed hibiscus tea. I reserve you the right to verify me, you so distant coming no closer, my life among the intransigentia.

My life as a polite notice: Please help keep this seat in a clean and tidy condition. Pearls ripped from hand-marrow. It wasn't you; what is irascible in us is distance. There is a stream, mist descending, malachites exhale and the palms of fish come up just to the grass. Half a desire, an entire phone card are some of today's stories.

My life envisioned among children: Not what you would make out behind a blind, floating in glaze, but children who were embryos, with history, a diet, throwing stones at each other behind the bus stop but intelligently in the spirit of exploration, unignorant of discourse, all process, breathing cereal at times and buying snakes.

My life as human geography: The 73 bus to Victoria boasts me as a bit of its architecture. I squirm, hallowed into cornice by the upper deck; the bus moves, complaining, to avoid being solved. What I am telling you is almost equal to vision. It has nothing to do with you pressed against me, in residence with me on this earth.

TEA LOUNGE ADVENTURE

The dragon kite passes a girl of indeterminate womanhood and salutes her. The wall waves its small rattan hands in time to the music. The couch smells like preserved shrimp paste; someone calls my name and now I too am shrimp paste. Yellow peppers line the floor. You are obviously your own complexion.

The woman of indeterminate girlishness will figure significantly in my story. Our group draws tighter; we met at stamp camp when we were of indeterminate emotional receptivity and squashed each other and exchanged birdbrained kisses. We initially bondaged over the Brazil and Oklahoma stamps, the one celebratory,

the other a pair of Christians, but it blossomed into so much more. At stamp camp we did not just lick but also sang and swung over lower Ausable Lake in a burning tire. Years later I would remember the moment my tongue met Kenya for the first time. All I could think was mintyfresh. But friends, it was not to be.

No, the incidence of youth was not to last. She indeterminate, I overdetermined, we agreed to part; found each other here yearlings later sipping monkeypicked and momentarily without our glossaries. Couldn't this have been done in an email or in an empty room in the forest? Give me your name. This time I'll hold it close.

OFFICE BY THE SEA

for R. B.

High in the office by the sea, we traded promises of chivalric fealty and worked through the agenda our parents had left for us. We were naive, having no knowledge of the virtue that lies in the mallow or the asphodel. The snowy plovers rejected our forays during protracted coffee breaks into their nests.

In those days I never went without handfuls of soap, another thing you understood. The line for pharmacopoeia and the one for deceit were each as long as dunes, and we held each other's place in them while learning to inflict love. We were offered mandrake, but it left us headachey and unyielding, like life.

The taste of self was on my tongue, your teeth capped with accusations. All you really wanted was the steel of my blood against your nails, and I knew that, so perhaps my love for you was a bit crazy. But it worked, as did your swelling breasts which I refused to acknowledge, knowing you wouldn't keep the baby.

After the forest fire, everything was different. Wooden fences ran at our approach and the lakes went orange. Gone were the tulips, the old country's abbreviations, those lovely dinners of forced meat. You told me you'd die a spinster with beautiful legs, then promptly got married, still fighting for custody over our abandoned flesh.

LEAN YEAR

Silence scooped out a hole in one eye and rested. A yellow calm descended on the cabin in the woods, its window yearning for insects. You know the one: next door to your brother, by the lake he kept in his pocket. His love of the Atlantic and its great living wires. As a child you rode through summers, abandoned me to cargo.

Then I was the happiest of the world's curs; you knew it and used it against me. You were so small that a boat could sail across you. You built a gourd for me; I blossomed like cellophane under your tutelage. The falsification of papers never happened to us, nor the story about how the rain walked across its stations.

Did you never regret the hyacinth fence? Did you hesitate before bucketing your sonnet, the night the trees realized they were electronic? We were directly connected, like a church and its ether. I only wished for more of the old square sofa and its stopped bodies. I regretted visiting the Hall of Nations.

Dear One: Life's good in the city. Breakfast on the Manitou Parkway, the green awnings of cars going by. If we lose something, we hunt for it, and if it wants us back, it cups its hands into parentheses. When we get bored, we value. Join me, won't you please? Given the white trees of fire, the gypsum's curtsey.

GRAIN IN EAR

This is what I saw and it does not have a name. After a week in which rain and snow fought over the city, someone wadded up a bunch of endings and shot them over the sea. They broke apart and fell down to the white tendrils of children and boats. A little God-light shafted the clouds, but that did not make it any easier.

Now is the half-month of Grain In Ear, beginning of June. To the south the rainy season begins to pry open the rice-heads. In the garden, writing at random, summer the tomato leaves. Villagers pound paper in the narrow lanes, or did once. A wanderer yawns to my interior stream, looks for his keys, departs.

I gather up my bones, their meticulous weight which I never notice. Memory is a thing Heaven and Hell have always shared – it is between them when they climb into bed at night and listen for the sea. I move farther down the row, to the bus with a hole in it. A suitcase flits across my neighbour's doorway, or perhaps a shard of salted fish.

It is a mistake not to think of the donkey contemplatives, their pens jagging over rice paper shrubs. One can't help but live when one has made it out, at least for now. Sound of a brush on concrete: small mammals prepare to dig up the season of peace. You and I are practically our own line of egrets. We breathe like roads.

THE WHITE HAPPINESS

When the monks draw breath, they become a way to skate on the creases of rocks. There it was, you again, the lost one. We walked away, holding the body that had been left us. The doctor tending the crops. Sadness is the kind of thing this house does not discuss. A song of paper. An opera written on the left thigh of a ghost.

The West Haven cabbages, renowned for their disappearance. The dragonfly with whom you fell in love. Of course I was the lost one, not you, marooned on the gurney. The column of breath, tallied and uncouth. Twelve breaths, four breaths, five. We might as well invite our teachers, the small cries of metal and stone.

Why do you think I am writing now? For you said, pressure this space. You said, everyone needs to be underwater. You said, I am dealing with growth. The punctured lung. The ways of taking leave. A boy in Hunan discovers rice in a folk song, puts on his hyaline coat. You said, what would it be like if I did not fear my body?

Here is a key aspect of ghost opera: when you are done, it is celebration, but no one is left. You find only the missing epinephrine. You craved ancestry, craved music. You said, go down and rejoice. You said, sitting outside a Paris café. Another aspect of ghost opera: it is never finished. It is the permission of summer.

NOTES

RAILROAD CAR WITH MOBILE PHONE AND MAN: "It is damn lonely… world" originates in the following quotation, attributed to "a person close to Crown Prince Abdullah" in "Saudi to warn Bush of rupture over Israeli policy," *New York Times*, April 25, 2002: "It is a mistake to think that our people will not do what is necessary to survive… and if that means we move to the right of bin Laden, so be it; to the left of Qaddafi, so be it; or fly to Baghdad and embrace Saddam like a brother, so be it. It's damned lonely in our part of the world, and we can no longer defend our relationship to our people."

ERRORS OF THE APOLLINARIANS: Cf. Augustine's *Confessions*: 7.19.

PERMITTED TO RETURN: This poem is for Douglas Kerr. The title is taken from Robert Duncan's *The Opening of the Field*.

D'OU VIEN DONC LE GRAND ASSEMBLY: The poem borrows lines from the unpublished 1705 recipe book and diary of Elizabeth Freke, housed in the British Library.

HOME and CHARLESTON STREET are one of three sets of "doublet" poems in the book (the others are "Windows Written in Youth" I and II and "Narrow Places"/ "Future Crocus." The procedure, which is drawn from Fanny Howe's "Introduction to the World," involves using one set of words in two different orders. 95% of the words in each of the pairs are the same.

WINDOWS WRITTEN IN YOUTH: "You who live... luck?" is from Robert Desnos, "Epitaph," trans. Kenneth Rexroth.

XERCES BLUE: In 1943, Xerces blue became the first documented butterfly species to become extinct in the United States. The poem refers to the Lobos Creek Dunes Restoration Project in San Francisco. Cf. "The City Goes Wild," *Orion Afield*, Spring 2002.

AIN HALEV: The title is Hebrew for "eye of the heart." In his *Mishneh Torah*, Maimonides writes, "You can never see matter without form, or form without matter.... Forms devoid of matter cannot be perceived by the eyes of the body but only by the eye of the heart. In the same way we know the Lord of the universe without physical vision."

STONES OF JERUSALEM originated in a lecture by Daniel Seidemann, founder of the Jerusalem-based NGO Ir-Amim.

CHEMICAL FIELD borrows and alters phrases from Charles Olson's "Projective Verse" and from Jeffery Goldberg's "The Great Terror," *The New Yorker*, March 25, 2002. The poem concerns Saddam Hussein's use of chemical weapons on the Kurdish city of Halabja, and was written before the second Gulf War. The last sentence is taken from *Twelfth Night*, I.i.5-6.

NARROW PLACES: It is traditional among Sephardic Jews to read *mitzrayim*, the

Hebrew word for Egypt, as *metzarim*, which means “narrow places.”

LAWS OF REST: Cf. *Mishnah Shabbat*, chapters 2, 7, and 8.

THE WHITE HAPPINESS is inspired by Tan Dun’s *Ghost Opera*. In the liner notes of the Kronos Quartet’s recording of the piece, the composer writes: “In Hunan… [d]eath was the ‘white happiness,’ and musical rituals launched the spirit into the territory of the new life.” This and the prior poem were written for Jordan Berlant.

ACKNOWLEDGEMENTS

I am grateful to those who read drafts and suggested invaluable revisions to this book along the way, especially Laura King, Grant Jenkins, Nathan Halverson, and Marianne Apostolides. Thanks to Rishma Dunlop and Priscilla Uppal for helping me navigate the Canadian publishing world.

A Works in Progress Grant from the Ontario Arts Council provided support for the manuscript's completion.

Thanks to Leo Mellinger Brubacher for delaying his arrival just long enough for his mother to finish the art for the cover.

Thanks to Jay and Hazel, for keeping literature alive in the most intellectually generous way possible.

Thanks to my parents, for their unfailing sanity and kindness, and to Mindy Stricke, for her steadfast support, artistic inspiration, and love.

Many thanks also to the editors of the following journals and anthologies, in which some of these poems first appeared: *6x6, Alice Blue, The Bedside Guide to No Tell Motel – Second Floor, Dusie, Jubilat, Listenlight, Octopus, The Paris Review, Pinstripe Fedora, Shampoo, Typo*, and *Zeek*.

ABOUT THE AUTHOR

DAVID B. GOLDSTEIN's poetry has appeared in journals and anthologies throughout North America. His translations appear in *The FSG Book of 20th-Century Italian Poetry*, among other publications. He is also the author of a chapbook from Dusie Press, and a book of literary criticism, *Eating and Ethics in Shakespeare's England*, as well as essays on a wide range of subjects, including Shakespeare, contemporary poetry, translation, food, philosophy, and domesticity. David lives with his family in Toronto, where he is Associate Professor of English at York University.

COLOPHON

Manufactured as the first edition of *Laws of Rest* in the fall of 2013 by BookThug.
Distributed in Canada by the Litereary Press Group: www.lpg.ca
Ditributed in the United States by Small Press Distribution: www.spdbooks.org
Shop online at www.bookthug.ca

BOOK
PRODUCTION
WAR ECONOMY
STANDARD

Type + design by Jay MillAr